FOUR LANE
AHMICI

```
A One Act Play By
Antony Jenkins
```

APS Books,
4 Oakleigh Road,
Stourbridge,
West Midlands,
DY8 2JX

APS Books is a subsidiary of the
APS Publications imprint

www.andrewsparke.com

Copyright ©2019 Antony Jenkins
All rights reserved.

Antony Jenkins has asserted his right to be identified as the author of this work in accordance with the Copyright Designs and Patents Act 1988

First published worldwide by APS Books in 2019

No part of this publication may be reproduced, stored in or introduced into a retrieval system, or transmitted, in any form, or by any means (electronic, mechanical, photocopying, recording or otherwise) without the written permission of the publisher except that brief selections may be quoted or copied without permission, provided that full credit is given.

A catalogue record for this book is available from the British Library

ISBN 978-1-78996-038-9

Set against the backdrop of the
Bosnian War, Four Lambs of Ahmiči
tells the story of four people
awaiting rescue from NATO. As the
Croatian and Serbian forces close
In around them, a single U.N
soldier must keep the peace between
three Survivors, one of which has a
deadly secret.

Four Lambs of Ahmiči was first
Performed in 2014 at Hereford's
Courtyard Centre for the Arts as
Part of the England Drama Festival
With the following cast:

U.N-   Ian Smith.
Old Man- David Thomas.
Nurse-   Katy Dalton.
Man-   William Moore

Directed by Anthony Jenkins
Sound   Richard Loveridge
Lighting   Sue Grenfell

Characters

U.N-	A British soldier in his mid-30s.
Old man-	A Serbian civilian in his late-60s.
Nurse-	A Croatian Nurse in her mid-20s.
Man-	A Bosniak soldier in his late teens.

*A derelict house in Ahmiči, Bosnia,
September 1992.*

*A tuning wireless crackles followed
by a cacophony of ITN and BBC news
reports about the conflict.*

Lights begin to flicker as a
*bombardment begins. Suddenly a
young girl dashes into the house
followed by a soldier dragging a
wounded man. An older man limps
behind after them. After a few
moments the bombing dies down but
continues faintly throughout the
piece. The soldier ransacks through
the house ripping down curtains
to make blankets. The Old man turns
and stands in the doorway staring
out.*

U.N-   (*To the old man*) No! No!
            Away! Stay away!

*He escorts the Old Man away from
the door. Suddenly a voice calls
out on the U.N radio.*

V/O-   **'Alpha 4?! Alpha One-
            Zero, do you copy over?'**

U.N-   Alpha One-Zero...this is
            Alpha 4 receiving you,
            over!

V/O—   '…**Reports of heavy fire in your area...What is your SITREP …over**'.

U.N—   Alpha One-Zero, SITREP is some bastard starting shelling as soon as the evacuation began! (*Wiping the sweat and trickle of blood from his forehead*) Transport's gone, we're scattered all over the place and the losses are many! I'm held up in a shack about half a mile south of the extraction point. I've got one man down, unresponsive. I've also two others, they're pretty beaten up but they're ok, request immediate pick up, over

V/O—   '…**Alpha 4, we advise you stay where you are! The Serbs have dug into the mountains to the west of you and are targeting civilian areas in the south!**'

U.N—   (To himself) Christ!

V/O—   '…**we can't risk a rescue at this time! Two patrols are pinned down in Bradina and Bosnian**

roadblocks are slowing down our convoys in Vitez! Major Lewis and the battalion are on their way to Ahmiči to organise a cease fire, he'll pick you up on the way back. Acknowledge so far, over'.

U.N- Alpha One-Zero I acknowledge, but what of the wounded?! Over!

V/O- **'…Alpha 4, just do the best you can at this time! Good luck, Alpha One-Zero out.**

U.N- (*To himself*) Fuckin' 'ell! (*Composes himself*) Ok…ok…does anyone speak English? (*They all stare*) Engleski? Anyone? Does anyone understand?

Nurse- Yes, I understand you.

U.N- Good! Ok, look my commander, my boss is gonna find whoever's bombing the place and get 'em to stop firing so we can...

Old man- Nije srpski!

U.N-   …what? What did you say?

Old man-   I heard you boy, it's not
            Serbians! It's not us
            U.N! It's those fucking
            murdering Croat pigs!

U.N-   Hang on a second, you
            heard what…

Old man-   Sranjé! Look around you!
            It is them I am telling
            you! Croats! Bastards!
            (*Indicating to outside*)
            Look what they're doing!
            Look what they're doing
            to the place! They've
            taken the hills and now
            they want the city!
            They're responsible for
            this (*screams to the
            outside world*) murdering
            bastards!

U.N-   Listen to me!
            (*Approaching him
            reassuringly*) I need you
            to calm down, ok?! Relax,
            take a breath! Just wait
            for…

Old man-   (*Shaking him off*) I
            cannot wait U.N! I've got
            to get out of here. I
            must get home!

U.N-   (*Steps in front*) I cannot allow that!

Old man-   What?! What do you mean 'you cannot allow'?!

U.N-   I cannot allow any of you to leave right now its suicide! Listen to it out there!

Old man-   This is my home U.N you've no right to order me!

U.N-   I'm not ordering…

Old man-   No right to come to my home and tell me when and where I can go!

U.N-   Listen to me, anyone who sets one foot out of here is dead do you understand me?! You speak English I'm sure you understand that word 'dead'! Yes?

Old man-   Fuck you U.N! My family needs me!

U.N-   You're family will see you again I promise! Just calm down!

Old man- (*Scoffs*) they could all
          be dead for all you know!

U.N-   You don't know that
          mate...

Old man- I am not your mate!

U.N-   Ok look, I give you my
          word your family are
          safe. Just wait until
          help arrives and we'll
          take you to them.

Old man- Jebi Se U.N!

*The Old man heads for the door the
U.N steps in front of him again,
there's a struggle and the U.N
pushes the Old Man back inside the
house.*

U.N-   You're not going
          anywhere!

Old man- I am not a prisoner!

U.N-   Shut up and listen! You
          walk out of here your
          family will never see you
          again! Get it?

Old man- I am Serbian boy! I'm
          safer than any of you!

The U.N stands firm and the old man

steps back.

U.N–   You're safer with me pal,
          I suggest you accept
          that.

*Old Man chuckles and walks away
mumbling to himself.*

Nurse–   When will your commander
          come?

U.N–   Soon. Here.

He offers cigarettes.

Nurse–   I'm sorry I don't.

*U.N offers a cigarette to the old
man who takes the whole packet and
sits in his corner. The U.N stares
in disbelief.*

Old man– What? You think a packet
          of cigarettes will make
          this any easier? Ha!

U.N–   I'm so sorry this has
          happened to you, to all
          of you, but we're here
          and I will not let
          anything happen to you so
          long as you co-operate
          with me…yes?

Old man– Sranje! You have promised
          many things in the past

U.N.

Nurse-   We would be dead if it
          wasn't for him.

Old man- Who asked you?!

U.N-   That's enough! Look, I'm
          in the same boat as you.
          I know how you feel, I
          wanna be back home with
          my feet up like the rest
          of you! But I can't, so
          make your peace with it.

U.N checks on the wounded man.

Old man- You are like us?

U.N-   What?

Old man- You say you are like us?

U.N-   I'm in the same boat yes.

Old man- Then you have no
          authority over me U.N!
          You are another refugee
          in a room. You're
          nothing!

U.N-   Look, enough of this
          shit! I'm here to help
          you and keep you from
          getting your fucking head
          blown off! You see this?
          It says 'United Nations',

                    peacekeepers, understand?

Old man chuckles and sarcastically
applauds.

Old man- You're doing well U.N (!)

U.N-   (*Quietly face to face*)
          Listen to me pal, you're
          in here alive and well
          because of us, because of
          me. Surely a little
          courtesy wouldn't go a
          miss 'mate'?! And even if
          you can't extend that
          courtesy how about you
          shut your trap for a bit
          before I shut it for you,
          eh?

The U.N turns and assists the
nurse. The distant gunfire
continues to crackle.

Old man- You don't understand
          'boy' this is my land, my
          home! I am free to go
          wherever I want!

U.N-   Excuse me, but haven't
          you noticed the shit
          that's going on lately?!
          You bastards are killing
          each other on a daily
          basis all because of
          'your land!' Snipers will
          just as easily kill you

                    as they would me or her.

Old man-   Croats would they don't
            care! Or Muslim. Soulless
            bastards!

U.N-   The world sees
            differently.

Old man-   The world doesn't care
            U.N.

U.N-   I'm living proof that it
            does!

Old man laughs.

Old man-   You?! (*Chuckles*) Bosnia
            calls for help and they
            send blue helmets and
            paperwork! You cannot
            fight you cannot shoot!
            You cannot do anything!
            They should have sent boy
            scouts instead.

U.N-   Our mandate is to shelter
            and protect.

Old man-   (*Chuckles*) you did well
            in Srebrenica! Isn't that
            right, U.N? Marched out
            by its' own people! When
            will you understand boy,
            you are not wanted here!
            Go! Leave! Leaves us in

                    peace! We can end this
                    without your help!

U.N-   Markale Market ring any
                    bells? Hm? Remember that?
                    Sixty people dead and
                    fuck knows how many
                    injured thanks to your
                    Serb brothers! Hundreds
                    came running up to us
                    with that look in their
                    eyes, wondering 'why?'
                    'Why is this happening?'
                    'What had they done to
                    deserve this?' I tell you
                    now pal, having a six-
                    year-old asking why I'm
                    sticking what's left of
                    his mother in a bin bag
                    is something the likes of
                    you will never
                    understand!

Old man-   That was Muslim shelling
                    Muslim!

U.N-   Bullshit! Serb Generals
                    even boasted about it!

Old man-   Don't believe everything
                    you see in the media boy!
                    Muslims are far worse!
                    And Croats? Well, they
                    eat their own.

U.N-   Bloody delusional
             propaganda.

*Old man grabs some dirt off the
floor.*

Old man-   Look...Serbian soil! Look
             U.N!

U.N-   (*Rifling through his
             bergen*) I'm dealing with
             other important matters
             at the moment.

Old man-   (*Gripping the dirt*)
             Serbian land. My land. We
             kill all who threaten to
             defile it. We fight to
             save ourselves!

U.N doesn't answer.

Old man-   ...UN?!

U.N-   How the fuck can a 6-
             year-old defile your
             land?! Huh?! There's no
             logic or reasoning behind
             your bloody brutality!
             Serbian or otherwise!
             Fucking beheadings and
             child rapings it's all
             lunacy! Barbaric!

Old man-   We've been doing it for
             centuries U.N, all the
             blue helmets in the world

```
                    cannot stop it.

U.N-        We can try.

Old man-    That's all you do boy is
            try! You cannot stop a
            nation defending itself.

U.N-        Jesus, give it a rest
            would you?

Old man-    Do you believe we Serbs
            will simply step aside
            and let Croatian pigs
            take our homes?! What
            would you do boy, huh?
            (U.N doesn't answer) You
            know I am right, don't
            you boy? You know I speak
            the truth. And that boy
            would have grown up to be
            like his father and we
            would be dragged back
            into this shit again.
            History repeating
            history.
```

The old man finds a stool and slumps in a corner away from the others. He draws a line in the dirt.

```
Old man-  My land.
```

The awkward silence is suddenly broken by the nurse.

Nurse-   Thank you. Thank you for
           being here.

U.N-   You're welcome.

Nurse-   You're very kind. Like
           Noah and this is your
           ark.

U.N-   More like a knackered
           canoe. How is he?

Nurse-   I think some of his ribs
           are broken, his right is
           broken, some deep cuts in
           both legs and he has a
           severe head wound. He's
           lucky to be alive.

Old man-   You call that lucky?

Nurse-   I've done all that I can,
           but he needs morphine.

U.N-   He's had my last shot,
           there's nothing else I
           can give him.

Nurse-   We must get him to a
           hospital.

Old man-   He's finished U.N.
           There's nothing left of
           him, put him out of his
           misery.

Nurse-   Please don't say that!

U.N-   Pay no attention to him.
           What's your name?

Nurse-   Maria Kadic.

U.N-   Ok Maria, I want you to…

Old man-   'Kadic'?

U.N-   …keep him warm and make
           sure he doesn't loose any
           more blood…

Old man-   'Kadic'?!

U.N-   …you seem to have a magic
           touch you're doing well.

Old man-   Did you say 'Kadic'?

Nurse-   Yes, I'm a nurse at the
           hospital.

Old man-   'Kadic' Croatian? No?

U.N-   She's a nurse that's all
           that matters here!

Old man-   You're a Croat? Kadic?!

Nurse-   I am.

U.N-   So what?

Old man-   She's the reason we're
           here U.N! Throw her out!

                    Let snipers deal with
                    her!

U.N steps in front of him.

U.N-   Don't start that shit
            again!

Old man-   You and I are in here
            because of her! She's
            probably a spy!

Nurse-   Please, I'm not a spy!

Old man-   She's a traitor U.N!
            She'll throw us to the
            wolves!

Nurse-   It's not true…

Old man-   We'll be carried out of
            here! She'll call her
            bastards down and they'll
            kill us all!

Nurse-   No I…

Old man-   She probably signalled to
            them to start shooting at
            us!

U.N-   For God sake she's not a
            spy, she's a civilian
            like you!

Old man-   Fuck her! She's nothing
            like me! Throw the bitch

out!

U.N-   What's happening here is
           not her fault!

Nurse-   Please believe me sir!
           I'm not a spy!

Old man-   Shut your mouth bitch!
           This is your doing! This
           is your fault!

*He attacks her, the U.N intervenes
and pins him against the wall.*

U.N-   Don't you touch her!

Old man-   On her side U.N?!

U.N-   I'm on no one's side.

Old man-   (*Spits at him*) Traitor!

U.N-   Shut up and listen to me!
           None of this is her
           fault. And as far as I'm
           concerned, she's keeping
           this boy alive. One more
           false move out of you and
           I won't be so civil, do
           you understand me?!

Old Man-   Izdajnik! You favour
           Croat whores U.N? You
           like little pigs? Go,
           take her side boy, but I

warn you, you will suffer
for this!

*The Old Man makes a vulgar gesture,
shrugs off the U.N and goes back to
his corner again.*

U.N-   Look, I get there isn't
            any trust left in this
            country, God knows I'll
            never know the reasons
            behind it all. But try to
            understand that I'm
            trying to help you here,
            all of you. Can we all be
            at peace for a moment?
            Hm? Whiskey?

U.N pulls out a hip flask.

U.N-   Bells. Good stuff.

*U.N pours some into a tin cup and
hands it to the old man, who after
a moment of hesitation takes a huge
swig.*

U.N-   Lovely stuff isn't it?

Old man spits.

Old man-   It's piss!

U.N-   This is all I drink back
            in England…my home in a
            bottle.

He offers the nurse she declines.

U.N-   Look, I know things look
        like shit, but I promise
        you both its only for a
        short time. Mint?

Offers her a mint.

Nurse- No thank you.

U.N-   I'm afraid I've nothing
        in the way of food.

Nurse- I'm not hungry.

U.N-   How long have you been a
        nurse Maria?

Nurse- Two years, I graduated
        before the war started
        and have worked in the
        hospital since. I also
        assist the Red Cross.

U.N-   Got any family?

Nurse- Yes *(Pulling out a
        photograph*) my Mother
        Maria, I'm named after
        her, my father Raif he's
        a doctor…and my
        brother...Tomas.

U.N-   He a doctor too?

Nurse-   ...A soldier.

Old man grunts in disgust.

Nurse-   He's only 16 a medic for
            the HOS. A very gentle
            soul. Beautiful boy. We
            haven't heard from him in
            some months, he wrote us
            every day then
            suddenly…nothing. In our
            church we pray and light
            candles each day for him.
            Every morning my father
            walks to the top of a
            hill behind our house and
            calls out to him…but
            there's no reply.

U.N-   When this is all over
            you'll have your Tomas
            back safe and sound, I'm
            sure of it.

Nurse-   Thank you.

Old man-   Sad, sad, sight.

U.N-   What now?

Old man-   It's bad enough you talk
            to her but to lie to so
            sweetly is cruel U.N.

U.N-   I'm giving her hope.

Old man-   He's probably dead in a ditch like most Croats.

U.N-   You don't know that.

Old man-   And you do? You don't even know where you are. How could you possibly know where he is?

U.N-   Don't listen to him Maria, your brother is fine I'm sure.

Nurse-   How do you know?

U.N-   …well…

The radio screeches to life.

V/O-   **'Alpha 4, Alpha One-Zero, are you receiving over?'**

U.N-   Thank god! This is Alpha 4 receiving…go ahead over.

V/O-   **'…Major Lewis is unable to reach you at this time. The roadblocks in your area are too dangerous for our convoys and the local militia will not cooperate! Acknowledge so far,**

over'.

U.N—   ((To himself) Jesus!
Alpha One-Zero, I
acknowledge but I'm need
of medical assistance,
surely the Major can
spare somebody?! Over.

V/O—   **'…Alpha 4, you must
understand that right now
we're flying blind! Safe
zones no longer
correspond with any of
our maps and casualties
on our side are
increasing! Major Lewis
is still in the process
of locating the Serbian
and Croat Generals to
organise this ceasefire
to get you out, but you
have to be patient! We're
spread too thin on the
ground to assist all
patrols! Just keep your
head down and we'll be
with you ASAP! Alpha One-
Zero, out.**

U.N—   Bastards!

*Silence (apart from the distant
shelling).*

Old man-   You are going to create a
           lot of paperwork boy.

U.N-   Bloody cowards! Bunch of
           cock sucking wankers!
           Call 'em selves
           soldiers?!

Old man-   There is no room for
           heroes boy, not in Amici!

U.N-   Shut up.

Nurse-   So...we wait here?

Old man-   You can. I know other
           ways home.

Nurse-   He won't last long U.N he
           needs a hospital!

Old man-   Put him out of his
           suffering. He won't feel
           anything.

Nurse-   Please don't say such
           things, he's just a boy!

Old man-   He's as good as dead U.N
           leave him.

Nurse-   NO! You can't leave him
           U.N! Please!

Old man-   Let's take care of the
           living for now boy, yes?

Nurse-   What shall we do? (*No answer*) U.N? What should we do?

U.N-   You heard my orders. We wait.

Nurse-   But he'll die if we don't get him...

U.N-   I KNOW!! I know the situation! But what can I do?! If we leave here we're all fucked! (*Pause*) No, we wait here for a patrol, that's our best chance, there aren't any other options!

Old man-   Nightfall, that is my option.

U.N-   Yeah? Then what? Fondle your way through bushes and razor wire and HOPE you don't step on a land mine?! What's your plan for running into Croatian hands, hmm? What's your 'plan' to prevent your head ending up on a fucking flagpole?

Old man-   All risks I'm willing to take.

U.N-   Then go! Just go! I'm
        tired of this! I've tried
        to make you realise
        what's happening out
        there but you're either
        to fucking dumb or
        stubborn to see sense! If
        either of you want to go,
        then go! Piss off! And
        best of luck to you.

Silence.

Nurse- I want to stay. Please.

U.N-   Well as Gandhi over there
        pointed out I've no
        authority here, so you're
        free to do whatever you
        want.

*He heads to the doorway and stares
out. Pause.*

Nurse- '*Fear not, for I am with
        you; be not dismayed, I
        will strengthen you, I
        will help you, I will
        uphold you with my
        righteous right hand*'. My
        mother often recites
        comforting words like
        that. Does that comfort
        you?

U.N-   Not really. But thank you
        for the effort.

U.N rifles through and checks his limited supplies. The old man rummages around the drawers and empty cases.

U.N-   Oi! I hope you're not looting?

Old man- Loot? What am I going to loot? The walls? Relax boy you worry too much. Find your peace.

The old man finds an old radio.

Old man- Ah! Some good after all! I promise I won't 'loot' it.

He then sits on his stool and switches it on. He tunes through the static until he hears an angelic folk song. For a moment the distant shelling is drowned out by the music and all is at peace. After a few moments the tune cuts out. EXPLOSION! Suddenly the boy gasps and comes too. U.N assists the nurse.

U.N-   Easy kid! You're ok! You're in safe hands. Don't move! Lay still!

He coughs violently and winces in pain.

U.N-   You're ok, you're safe.
Breathe kid, breathe,
shhhh.

Nurse-   *Govoris Li Engleski?
Croat? Huh? Croat?*

U.N-   English? Can you
understand us?

Man-   (*Gasping*) Yes…W…What…what
hap…?

U.N-   It's ok you're alright
you're safe now.

*The man tries to move and grunts in
pain.*

Nurse-   Please try not to move.

Man-   Who, who, who are you?

U.N-   It's ok, just relax. This
is Maria she's been
looking after you since
we got here.

Man-   W…where?

U.N-   We're in Ahmici,
somewhere. We're waiting
for my guys to come and
take us home.

Old man- Yeah sure (!)

U.N-   They're coming! What's
          your name mate?

Man-   R…Rah…Rahmo J…Jamil.

Old man- Bosniak?

Man-   Y…Yes.

Old man- (*Chuckling and applauds*)
          Oh U.N you have a full
          house!

U.N-   Shut up!

Old man- You've the whole country
          in one room U.N. Let's
          see if you can do better
          than NATO.

U.N-   That's enough!

*Man doesn't answer he's in too much
pain.*

U.N-   You're a civilian yes?

Old man- Or a spy?!

U.N-   Will you shut up?!

Man-   Min fadlik…please my head
          I cannot…

Old man-   I agree with the boy, you
            bark too much U.N.

U.N-   Just piss off back to
            your corner!

Old man-   More snakes in the room
            U.N. Be warned.

Nurse-   Please! Can I suggest
            that we should relax a
            little now? The boy is
            awake and we're all
            alive! We should thank
            God for this.

Old man-   Oh yes thank God (!)
            Praise God (!) Praise him
            for putting us all in
            this shit in the first
            place!

Nurse-   God is with us I know it!

Old man-   How do you know? Can you
            see him?!

Nurse-   He bought you here
            safely.

Old man-   YOU bought me here you
            crazy bitch! You're not
            God! There is no God!

Nurse-   I tell you, he saved us!

Old man-   He no longer cares! He
           has forgotten us!

Nurse-   He's watching over us,
           even you.

Old man-   Yeah sure (!) You
           positive we cannot throw
           her out?!

U.N-   That's enough!

Man-   Min yatruk…Min…I must go,
           I must leave (*Grunts in
           pain*)

U.N-   No, no, no stay still!
           Don't move! Ok, Maria is
           going to watch over you.

Nurse-   Where are you going?

U.N-   I'm making a call and
           getting everyone out of
           here. This changes
           everything!

Man-   La! No! Please…

*He tries to rear up but is
paralysed by the pain and is
immediately cradled by Maria.*

Nurse-   You must lie still. Are
           you sure you can't give
           him anything?

U.N-   I told you I've nothing
           left. Just keep him warm
           and try not to excite
           him.

*The man begins to cry in pain. U.N
attempts to make a call but the
signal has gone.*

Nurse-   Shhh, its ok I am with
           you. God is with you.

*She continues to wipe his brow and
make him more comfortable.*

Nurse-   (*Prays quietly*) *Heavenly
           Father I pray you take
           this boys pain away and
           let him rest in peace,
           for he has been wounded
           by those who have
           strayed, I pray you send
           comfort and serenity...*

Old man-   Ohh stop your tongue
           Croat, please.

Nurse-   *...This I ask in the name
           of the father, the son
           and the Holy Ghost, amen.*

Old man-   (*Dropping to his knees*)
           Oh God, oh merciful, all
           loving, almighty God I
           pray, no, I BEG that you
           shut this woman up! For

35

she is driving your flock
insane…

Silence.

Old man-   (*Surprised*) Thank you (!)

U.N-   Shit! (*Thinking
            frantically*)

Nurse-   What is it?

U.N-   The signal is too weak to
            make proper contact.

Nurse-   But you spoke to your
            men, we heard you.

U.N-   Signals come and go. Most
            of the time it's just
            guess work.

Nurse-   What do we do?

U.N-   (*Indicates to the outside
            world*) gotta stick my
            head out there. It's our
            best chance.

Nurse-   But what you said about
            snipers? They could shoot
            you.

U.N-   There's enough cover out
            there, should be fine.
            Besides, if I don't make
            it back you're free to do

whatever you want. (*Looks at the Old Man*) aren't ya? I'll be right back.

He leaves.

Old man-   Arrogant foolish boy! Budala! You know, if I were dying and you were whining, I'd beg God to take me.

Nurse-   All I have left is hope and faith what's wrong with that?

Old man-   You're wailing brings nothing.

Nurse-   It brings me peace.

Old man-   You're too loud with it! And you spit it like a snake!

Nurse-   If I could climb the tallest spire and scream to him I would.

Old man-   Why don't you try it? You'd make an easy target.

Old man grunts.

Nurse-   I have never met you before and yet you talk

37

to me with spite. Why is
that? Do I look like a
soldier? Do I look like I
could hurt an old man
like you? No…I have been
taught to love and to
cherish. That is me. That
is who I am. You'll never
change that. You'll never
change me.

Old man-   Nor me.

Nurse-   Then why do you tell me
to 'stop praying' and to
'stop believing' when you
know I'll never listen?!
There are hundreds,
thousands like me still
holding onto hope.

Old man-   You're fools to think
some angel will float
down and save you.
Madness! It's nothing
personal, although I
cannot stomach the sight
of you.

Nurse-   I almost feel sorry for
you.

Old man-   Don't.

Nurse-   Why are you such an angry
man?

Old man-   Angry because I'm trapped
           in this house with you! I
           should be at home! I
           should be with my family!
           Not in here listening to
           YOU! FUCK YOU!

Nurse-   Ok I'm sorry! Please
           don't be angry I was just
           trying to make you see
           I'm not your enemy. I
           didn't mean to upset you
           I'm sorry.

*She goes to touch him. He backs
           away.*

Old man-   When will you learn that
           help from heaven never
           comes, girl?

Nurse-   You sound so sure of
           that.

Old man-   Why am I talking to you?
           I don't know you you are
           nothing to me so why am I
           still in the same room
           talking to you?!

Nurse-   Because I am listening.
           That's how it works isn't
           it? You talk I listen.

Old man is (for once) speechless.

Nurse-   (*Softly*) Can I ask...why
              are you so certain? Why
              are you so sure help will
              never come?

Old man sits quietly for a moment.

Old man-   Croat (*Pause*) girl. God
              supports the wicked,
              history has shown us
              that. You see it even
              today.

Nurse-   Not always.

Old man-   We had a Croat neighbour
              by the name of Gideon, he
              was a priest and a
              teacher, everyone loved
              him and attended every
              service. And in 1944 he
              threw it all away to save
              his own skin. Sunday
              morning came, we flocked
              to his church eager to
              hear 'the word of God'
              but instead we were met
              by the Ustasi. (*He takes
              a moment*) Gideon stood at
              his pulpit and read out
              every name every creed.
              And he watched as those
              named were herded onto
              trucks like sheep. I saw
              my entire neighbourhood
              die in the house of God.
              I watched my mother and

father kneel at Gideon's feet, arms stretched pleading to him, pleading to spare us, pleading to God. I tell you girl, there was no answer that day, no floating angel, no mercy, instead they were met with rifle butts (*Pause*) once the segregation was over, Gideon was also thrown onto a truck. They all went to the same place this I'm certain (*Pause*) Jasenovac. I along with two others were saved because we were strong and able. (*Chuckles to himself briefly*) so let me ask you this girl if a million people didn't get an answer, what chance do you think you have?

Nurse-   I'll never stop trying.

Old man walks up to her and kneels next to her.

Old man- Give up girl. Man is the only true God.

As he gets up he spots the watch on Rahmo's wrist.

Old man- You know you can spot a
          Bosniak pig a mile off?
          By his jewellery. Cheap,
          loud shit.

*Nurse gently takes the wrist and
inspects the watch.*

Nurse-   My Tomas had a watch like
          this.

Old man- Your Tomas had no taste.

*U.N enters. Nurse continues to
inspect the watch.*

U.N-   Ok, good news! From what
          I could make out both
          Croats and Serbs are
          aware of NATO's presence
          in Ahmici.

Old man- And yet they still shoot
          at you?

U.N-   Look, they've both agreed
          to a ceasefire or at
          least give us some time
          to evacuate.

Old man- And then what?

U.N-   We make for a new safe
          zone outside Vitez.

Old man- What of me? What of my
          family?

U.N–   We're moving everybody
          out of Ahmici so you'll
          meet them in Vitez.

Old man– You are sure?

U.N–   I promise.

Old man–   How long will it take?

U.N–   It's all happening as we
          speak. Best bloody news
          I've had all day (!)
          First thing I'm gonna do
          is have a brew.

Old man– 'Brew?'

U.N–   Yeah brew ya know? Cup of
          tea.

The conversation is cut short by
the nurse staring down at Rahmo.

Nurse–   Where is he?! Where is my
          Tomas? Please tell me
          Rahmo where is my
          brother!

U.N–   Hey, hey what's wrong?

Nurse–   Where is he?!

U.N–   What's wrong? Maria what
          is it?

Nurse-   This is my brother's
          watch!

U.N-   What? How can you be
          sure?

Old man- Plenty of shit like that
          on the markets.

Nurse-   It's his I swear to you!
          Look…it has his initials
          on the strap those are
          his! It's Tomas'! Where
          is he?!

U.N-   Calm down Maria, calm
          down. (*Gently*) Rahmo?
          Rahmo can you hear me?

Nurse-   (*Frantic*) Wake up please!

U.N-   Stand back Maria!

Old man moves her back.

U.N-   Rahmo can you hear?!

Rahmo comes too.

U.N-   Rahmo…this watch? You see
          it? Is it yours?

Man-   W…what...

U.N-   This watch? Is it yours?

Man-   Y...yes.

U.N-   You are sure Rahmo?

Man-   It is mine.

U.N-   He says it's his Maria.

Nurse-   If that is true then what
          do these letters mean to
          you?

Man-   Madha, w…what…what
          letters?

Nurse-   These! (*Becoming
          desperate*) These letters!
          These letters! 'T.K' what
          do they mean? What do
          they mean to you?!

Rahmo groans in pain and mumbles.

Nurse-   They're my brother's
          initials! They're his I
          swear it! Where did you
          get his watch Rahmo?!
          Please? PLEASE!

Man tries to roll away.

Nurse-   (*Slamming back down he
          screams*) Where is my
          brother?!

Man-   'Idi do djavola' (*He
          grunts in pain and*

frustration) I want to go.

Nurse-   (Shaking him) tell me!

U.N-   Hey back off! The boy says it's his! You must be mistaken Maria. I'm sorry.

Nurse-   I tell you he knows where he is U.N! Believe me, I tell you he knows!

U.N-   Maria look at him, the kid hasn't a clue what day it is! Look, I understand you're upset but you can't blame every bloke you come in contact for your brother's disappearance.

Old man rifles through Rahmo's shoulder bag.

Man-   La! No! No please!

Old man-   Something you missed U.N?

U.N and Old man check his contents Maria sits in a corner clutching her brother's watch.

Man-   No! Do…Do not take my bag…no!

U.N-   We're just checking for
          I.D mate, nothing to
          worry about, just relax.

Old man pulls out a hand full of
watches and gold chains.

U.N-   What the f…?

Old man- Souvenirs boy? Hm?

U.N-   What do you mean?

Old man- I know what these are
          U.N! Souvenirs Rahmo?
          Yes?

Man-   Jebi Se! Allaenat ealayk!
          Do not take my bag!

U.N-   Souvenirs? What do mean
          souvenirs?!

Old man steps on his leg. Rahmo
screams.

Old man- Taken from the dead, boy?
          That what you did?

The U.N pulls him away.

U.N-   Leave him! What the hell
          do you think you're
          doing?!

Man-   Bastard! Allaenat ealayk!

Old man-   These are taken from the
            dead U.N! That's how
            'looting' works yes?!
            This bastard probably
            stole them once they lay
            dead am I right?! Am I
            right boy?!

*Old man stamps on Rahmo's leg again
and the U.N shoves him away.*

U.N-   Stop it! How could you
            possibly know that?

Old man-   (*Old man pulls his sleeve
            up to reveal a tattooed
            number on his underarm*)
            because I've seen it! I
            tell you he took these
            from the dead, probably
            from those camps.

Nurse-   What camps?

U.N-   Detaining camps.

Old man-   Death camps! He's
            Bosniak, yes? He probably
            got these from Hrasnica
            or Celebici! I've heard
            about them. I've heard
            they're run by cruel
            bastards.

Nurse-   Death camps? Oh God no is
            that true?

U.N- No it's not true! Just
more of his bloody
paranoid gossip! They're
holding camps, detaining
camps, that's all.

Old man- You know what goes on
inside those barracks,
boy.

U.N- Oh come on there isn't
any evidence to suggest
that! Just rumours that's
all! Death camps are
extinct, the Geneva
Convention prohibits it!
So don't go putting faith
into such rubbish.

*Old man chuckles in disbelief, he
then dumps all the watches and gold
chains into the
U.Ns hands.*

Old man- Prohibits? Prohibits you
say? Well there is your
evidence U.N! There is
your proof! Each one
soaked in blood! Maybe
you should put more faith
in your eyes than your
Geneva Convention huh?!

Nurse- Could…could Tomas be in
one of those camps?

U.N- No I…I don't know.

Nurse-   Rahmo? Please, I'm
             begging you, where is my
             brother is. (*She shows
             her photograph*) He's a
             medic in the Territorial
             Army. He's only a boy!
             Please, have you seen
             him?!

Man doesn't answer.

Nurse-   (*To the U.N*) Please help
             me.

U.N-   I'll try but you need to
             calm down.

He gently escorts away from Rahmo.

U.N-   Rahmo I need you to
             listen to me kid. I need
             to know where you got
             this watch. It's
             important! I'm not
             interested in the rest of
             your swag, I just need to
             know about this. Tell me.

Man-   I f…found it.

Old man-   You found them all boy
             huh?!

U.N-   Quiet!

Rahmo grunts in pain.

U.N-   Look Rahmo, I suggest you
            do yourself a favour mate
            and tell us the truth.
            Otherwise we'll find out
            when we get back.

Man-   Jebi se U.N!

U.N-   What did he say?

Old man-   'Go fuck yourself'.

Nurse-   Please Rahmo!

Old man-   Try the Serbs! They'd cut
            him in ways that would
            make him talk! Or why not
            take him to meet your
            mother girl, huh? She
            would get her answers
            like that! (*He claps his
            hands*)

Nurse-   (*Softly*) Please Rahmo?

U.N-   I won't ask again kid.
            Vitez will be full of
            Croats when we get back,
            I'm sure they'll be happy
            to help.

Nurse-   (*Desperately*) Please.

She holds the photo to his face.

Man-   (*He stares at Maria*) I…I
              did see him…

Nurse-   You did?! Where? Where
              did you see him?

Man-   Celebici…some days ago. I
              was a 'nothing' a simple
              munazzaf, a cleaner…
              But…I was made to do
              other things.

U.N-   Like what?

Man-   Digging, burying…getting
              rid of shit. Dirty job!
              Shit job! Made me sick!
              Th…then I was made to
              bury the dead…

Old man-   (*Whispering into his ear*)
              told you U.N.

Man-   First it was the sick,
              dead from disease. Then
              it was those who tried to
              escape, punishment…then…

U.N-   …then?

Man-   Then it was those killed
              for fun. That was just
              the men the women and
              children had it much
              worse. Ethnic cleansing
              is growing. Wiping out
              the young is essential

now. We will not let the future live.

U.N-   (*To himself*) Jesus Christ.

Man-   Everyone knows what goes on in those camps.

U.N-   (*Quietly to himself walking away*) I can't believe what I'm hearing. Just can't fucking believe it! (*Pulls himself together*) how did you get all this gear?

Man-   They didn't need them anymore. I took what I could and ran. I wanted to get out I wanted money, I HATE this place! I hate my home! My country! I hope it all burns!

Nurse- (*Exhausted*)…my brother?! Where's my Tomas?

Man-   He…h…he tried to escape.

Nurse- …what…

Man-   They thought he was a spy…like all men in Bosnia, they are not to be trusted (pause)…I remember him.

Nurse-   …d…dead?

Man-   (*Pause*) yes. Along with Sarajevo.

Maria crumples.

U.N-   (*Still in disbelief*) you little bastard.

Man-   Idi u pakao! I was doing my part! Why don't you take your tanks to Celebici and do yours!

He gasps in pain.

Man-   …I could…mushhhka…anymore…I…

He blacks out. A stunned silence fills the room.

Old man-   So…what do you want to do?

U.N, still in shock, doesn't answer.

Old man-   U.N?

U.N-   What?

Old man-   What do we do with him?

U.N-   I wished I left him in
         the road. (*Composes
         himself*) We'll take him
         back…let the Hague deal
         with him.

Old man- You are in charge boy.

U.N-   I can't believe a kid of
         his age could… (*still in
         shock*) Jesus Christ.

Old man- This is war U.N, the
         world has gone to hell.

U.N-   Maria…I'm so very sorry.
         If there's anything…

Nurse-   There's nothing.

*She puts on her brothers watch and
sits in a corner and closes her
eyes. The old man takes his jacket
off and wraps it around her. The
radio screeches to life and a faint
voice is heard.*

V.O-   …**Alpha…Alpha Four…This
         is…One…**(*Static*)

U.N-   Alpha One-Zero this is
         Alpha four can you hear
         me? Over?

Radio crackles.

55

U.N-   Shit! I've gotta get a clearer signal! This could be our rescue! I'll be back!

Old man- Go, go.

U.N leaves.

Old man- (*To himself*) What a fucking day. There's nothing that you or I can say that will bring your brother back. You have my sympathies.

He wanders around and places the watches and gold chains back in Rahmo's shoulder bag. He kneels next to Rahmo.

Old man- You brainless boy. How could you think you could escape hell with a sack full of rings? You'll never escape Bosnia boy, believe me I've tried. You are as damned as the rest of us. These belong with their owners. I'm going to give them back.

He leaves. Rahmo briefly comes around and mumbles incoherently. Maria stares at him from a distance. Distant explosions continue.

Man-   Mama...Mummm...I don't...Where
            am...

Nurse-   So you remember him? Moj
            brat?

Rahmo continues to mumble faintly.

Nurse-   And you buried him? You,
            a child put him in the
            ground. (*Wipes her eyes*)
            It's strange...I should
            feel strong hatred and
            disgust for you...but even
            as I look at you now...the
            only feeling I have...is
            pity.

*Rahmo groans then slips into
unconsciousness again, Maria crawls
over and sits next to his head and
talks to him while gently stroking
his head.*

Nurse-   Poor Rahmo. You poor poor
            boy. I wish I could
            understand. How can a boy
            do such things? What kind
            of Mother would allow her
            son to grow into such a
            monster? When did you
            realise you were capable
            of this Rahmo? God help
            me I'll never ever
            understand how such
            cruelty can be endured.

To stomach it so easily!
How can God allow it? But
then war isn't declared
in the name of God is it?
It's all man entirely.
Why? Why me? What have I
done to deserve this? I
have done you no wrong
and this is what I am
given in return…how can
this be? Am I missing
something? I don't want
to know what you did. I
don't want to know how
many you buried or how
old they were my thoughts
are already horrified!
Why me? I no longer have
a family because of you.
You...a boy...a kid an
infant son of a whore
have snatched it away
from me! And for what?
For what Rahmo?! All my
life I've been good,
tried to be fair and
forgiving and this is my
reward? How? How can this
be?! Because of you and
your brothers, because of
your kind you have taken
every ounce of hope away
from me! You murderer!
(Slaps him) You pig!
(*Slaps him*) You monster!
(*Pulls his hair in anger*)
You bastard! How could

you?! Why?! If you can
take a life so easily…so
can I. Maybe it's easier
than it looks.

*She covers his mouth with one hand
and pinches his nose with the
other, he struggles and dies. She
lays his head down in peace. Old
man enters with dirty hands.*

Old man- Now the dead can have
their belongings in
paradise. Christ! Listen
to me 'paradise'! Maybe
someone can convert in
times of stress? Maybe
this what you believers
mean when you say 'God
works in mysterious way'?

No answer.

Old man- Soon we'll be free from
this dungeon. Soon we'll
be home with our… (*Pause*)
I am truly sorry for your
loss. Truly. Maybe it's
better if you flee this
shit country. Never look
back. Make new brothers.
Maybe our U.N friend will
take you home with him?
(*Looking at Rahmo*) and
you boy, maybe one day
you'll teach the world a
lesson.

The Old man soon realises Rahmo is not breathing.

Old man- …boy? Boy?!

The Old man shakes the boy.

Nurse-   A life for a life.

Old man- (*Pause*) What?

Nurse-   A life for a life.

Old man- What do you mean? What have you…?

Looks at Rahmo.

Old man- Oh girl what have you done?

Nurse-   (*To herself*) God forgive me.

Old man- What did you do?!

Nurse-   I had to do it.

Old Man- …oh no!

Nurse-   '*Then the LORD saw that the wickedness of man was great in the earth, and* (*Old man turns and slaps her*)…"

Old man-   You dumb bitch! You dumb
            fucking Croat!

Nurse-   (*Silencing him with her
            scream*) What was I
            supposed to do? My
            brother's killer lay at
            my feet and I'm supposed
            to help him?

Old man-   Girl you…

Nurse-   The bible says an eye
            for...

Old man-   You made a decision like
            that because of some
            fucking book?! You
            stupid…

Nurse-   You have Gideon lying at
            your feet, you know what
            he is and what he's done.
            What would you do? Let
            him go? Mend his wounds
            and send him on his way?
            Or as you say 'put him
            out of his misery'?

Old man-   Gideon got what he
            deserved, he betrayed us!

Nurse-   Take a look at me! I was
            betrayed! I had
            everything ripped away
            from me (*Softly*) 'An eye
            for an eye'.

Old man-   But you're only a child.

Nurse-   So was my Tomas. You look
           at me now, you look at me
           and tell this boy was fit
           to live after what he
           did! You tell me, you
           tell me! (*The Old man
           doesn't answer*) You
           cannot, you cannot and
           you know you cannot.

Old man-   After this…you are no
           different than he was.

U.N enters.

U.N-   Bastards! Fuck it!
           (*Composes himself*) The
           convoy is here.

Old man-   But that is good yes?

Pause.

U.N-   I have my orders to take
           out the seriously
           wounded…

Old man-   We know that U.N!

U.N-   …only.

Old Man-   What…what do you…?

U.N-   The trucks are already
          packed.

Old man- So? What are you saying?

U.N-   I can't…I can't take you.
          I can only take the
          wounded. I'm sorry. You
          have to make your own way
          to Vitez. (*Pause*) I'm so
          sorry, I tried to reason
          with them I tried
          everything! I begged
          them! I'm so sorry.

*Rumbling from tanks and gunfire
from outside.*

Nurse-   What's that?

U.N-   Croats have entered the
          city. Everyone has to
          leave now!

Nurse-   But you said they were
          upholding a ceasefire.

U.N-   Croats agreed to it just
          so they could reclaim the
          town without any
          casualties. Any non-
          Croatans found in the
          area are in serious
          trouble.

Old man- …like me?

U.N-   Look, I've had a thought,
           if you stay close to the
           convoy, I could keep an
           eye on you and…

Old man-   I can't run alongside a
           truck U.N!

Nurse-   What if we stay here?
           Could you come back for
           us?

U.N-   It could be weeks before
           we come back, I can't
           make that promise. If you
           were to hide you might…

Old man-   And I am not going to
           hide like some animal
           boy! I've done that
           before. Let luck decide.

U.N-   Jesus, I'm so sorry. I
           begged! I begged them to
           reconsider! But there are
           rules. I couldn't do
           anymore. I'm only allowed
           to take him. (*Nurse and
           Old man exchange a look.
           U.N becomes frantically
           desperate*) Here! Take all
           my cigarettes and my
           whiskey! Take my money!
           Take it all! Use them to
           barter, you do that here!
           They'll get you somewhere
           safe I'm sure of it!

Nurse-   I could speak for you?

U.N-   You can! Yes you can!
           Maria you're Croatian
           you're safe here! You can
           talk you can negotiate!
           You could vouch for him!

Old man-   I'm in no mood for
           talking with liars…or
           murderers.

U.N-   No please you must listen
           to me! Please I'm begging
           you! Let Maria talk for
           you! She won't let
           anything happen to you.
           She's the kindest woman
           I've met. Please! You can
           do this! She'll look
           after you. Won't you
           Maria?! Rahmo! Rahmo wake
           up mate you're on your
           way out of here. Rahmo
           come on! Rahmo wake up
           please!

He gently shakes him.

U.N-   Stop messing around
           Rahmo! Come on get up!

*He puts his head to Rahmo's chest
…nothing.*

U.N-   Oh no...oh god no! Rahmo!
            Oh come on son!

*U.N begins to pump on the Rahmo's
chest counting to himself then
blowing in his mouth.*

U.N-   Come on! (*Pause*) please,
            please! Don't just
            fucking sit there! Help
            me!

Continues to perform CPR.

U.N-   Oh come on! Come on son!
            Please Rahmo! Jesus
            Christ no, please!

Old man-   He's gone U.N let him be.

U.N-   No! (*Whispering to
            himself*) Not this boy.
            Please God not this boy.

Old man-   Boy, let him go! He's
            dead. Nothing you can do.

U.N stops and hangs his head.

U.N-   Give me a fucking break!

V/O-   **'Alpha four? This is
            Major Lewis! Are you
            receiving over?'**

U.N doesn't answer.

V/O– '...**Alpha four are you receiving? This is Major Lewis, over**.

U.N– (*Composes himself*) Major Lewis, this is Alpha four go ahead, over.

V/O– '...**You have to meet me at your previous location now in order to achieve extraction, over**.'

U.N– (*To himself*) I can't do this. Please God don't make me do this.

V/O– '...**Alpha Four did you copy? Acknowledge, over?**'

U.N– Major Lewis, can an exception be made on transporting two able bodied refugees, over?

V/O– '...**Orders are not to transport any refugees at this time. Wounded civilians and U.N personnel only, no refugees, over**.'

U.N– Christ! Major Lewis, my wounded has recently passed away. Could we substitute his place for a live civilian? They

could even take my place?
Over.

V/O-   '...**Alpha Four, this is
no time for sentiments
this comes from the
Colonel! You have five
minutes Alpha Four, out.**

U.N-   I tried. (*In pain*) God
help me I tried! Please
forgive me I tried…

Old man- Boy, you can try and try
but you'll never stop
hatred like this. I've
seen it many times and it
never stops burning. War
can make the purest angel
into a monster (*looks at
Maria*). Revenge boy,
revenge is too blinding.

U.N-   (*Looking at Rahmo*) God
help me I didn't want
this. I didn't want to
leave a failure.

Old Man- When you leave my country
boy, don't think of it as
a failure, think of it as
a lesson, as a warning.

U.N-   I'll leave and never give
this place a minute's
thought.

Old man-   ...then I'll see you
            again U.N.

Radio screeches to life.

V/O-   '...**Alpha Four...this is
            Major Lewis...we're ready
            to leave...you must leave
            your current location and
            meet me now! Over!'**

U.N-   Major Lewis, Alpha Four,
            I'm on my way, out.

He indicates for Maria to leave.

U.N-   What's your name?

Old man-   What difference would it
            make?

*Cheering voices and distant gunfire
in the distance. U.N leaves. After
a moment Maria leaves. The old man
follows them to the door way and
watches the convoy pull away.
Suddenly the radio comes to life,
the old man heads over and sits
next to it. Another angelic tune
plays as all hell is breaking loose
outside. The Old Man clutches his
radio and shuts his eyes.*

                        Black out.

```
SCRIPTS FROM APS BOOKS
      (www.andrewsparke.com)
```

Michael Harvey *A Shattered Rose*
Michel Henri *Twenty Pieces Of Silver*
Antony Jenkins *Four Lambs Of Ahmici*
John Wright *Sixteen Screenplays*

Printed in Great Britain
by Amazon